Do ana Understand

50 action stories for young learners

Günter
Gerngross

•

Herbert
Puchta

LONGMAN

Addison Wesley Longman Limited
Edinburgh Gate, Harlow, Essex, CM20 2JE, England, and Associated Companies throughout the world.

© in the original edition by ÖBV Pädagogischer Verlag GmbH., Vienna 1994

This edition © Addison Wesley Longman Limited 1996

This edition first published 1996 by arrangement with ÖBV Pädagogischer Verlag GmbH.

Third impression 1998

Illustrated by Svjetlan Junakovic, Zagreb

Cover illustration – Derek Matthews

Produced for the publishers by Sally Henry

Set in Helvetica

Produced through Longman Malaysia, ACM

ISBN 0582 29896 2

Contents

Introduction

1 What is Do and Understand?

Do and Understand is a collection of 50 short stories, to be used in the classroom with children aged 9 to 13. **Do and Understand** is an ideal supplement to any main course book or teaching material for this age range. The material has been designed to be flexible. The stories can be taught in any order, although the order they are listed in follows an "easy to more difficult" progression, according to vocabulary, sentence length and story length. The first stories are very simple and can be introduced after just a few hours of class.

Each story consists of a teacher's script (see pages 18 to 25), and two photocopiable worksheets - a cartoon picture story, and an activity worksheet (see pages 26 to 125).

The highly successful methodological approach in **Do and Understand** draws on the latest insights into learning coming from research into cognitive psychology and language pedagogy. These are summarised in the section **How do Children Learn?** on page 4.

Step-by-step guidance for working with the stories in **Do and Understand** is given in the section **Teaching with Do and Understand**, starting on page 6. In this section, you will find techniques for the introduction of vocabulary, and suggestions for how to tell a class a story in such a way that your pupils definitely understand it. You will also find options for working further with a story in class, in ways that it remains anchored in the children's long-term memory. This includes guidance for using the practice worksheets supplied in **Do and Understand**.

2 How do children learn?

2.1 How do children learn to talk in the mother tongue?

It is not unusual for children who live in areas (or homes) where two or more languages are spoken to learn each of these languages easily. Such a natural learning atmosphere can hardly be compared with that of the typical foreign language classroom. Still, it is worth taking a look at the factors that influence the acquisition of the mother tongue so we can understand how these may be put to good use in the teaching of a foreign language.

The acquisition of the mother tongue begins at birth, with the development of receptive language skills (listening) coming before productive skills (speaking). Children can understand words long before they begin to speak.

The new-born child first perceives language as a torrent of sounds. He/she then learns to filter words and their meanings out of this torrent. It is only then, when the listening skills are sufficiently developed, that the child will begin to express himself/herself verbally.

Adults naturally behave with young children in a way that facilitates the development of listening skills. Most importantly, we speak with them in such a way that they can understand what we are saying. The language we use must be clear and concrete and have a direct connection to the child's world. No one would even think of talking about abstract topics with a young child.

For example, we regularly give children instructions such as: Put the red car in the toy box next to the door. We repeat these kind of instructions time and time again, and often they are varied. An example of a variation would be: Put the yellow car in the bag next to the closet. If the child carries out an instruction, this proves that he/she has understood it, and he/she is praised.

Constant repetition, a stress-free, play-like learning atmosphere and frequent positive reinforcement are the most significant characteristics of this early phase of receptive learning.

Picture books, stories, rhymes and songs also play an important part in the acquisition of language. For example, the mother or father flips through a picture book with the child and reads the words while the child points at the corresponding pictures. Eventually children start to repeat words, phrases and then whole sentences. The repetitive reading of the same stories encourages the child (with the help of the pictures in the book) to learn the text with the parent, and finally, to recite parts of the text or the whole text by heart. The result is that even adults can still remember certain stories, which they heard over and over again in their childhood.

In summary, one can say that the training of listening comprehension skills is a deciding factor in the acquisition of the mother tongue. Concrete instructions, real objects and pictures support this learning process. They are important "memory anchors". With their help, children can retain better and recall more easily words and sentences that they continuously hear.

2.2 Teaching children a foreign language

Every age group has specific needs when learning a foreign language. Children learn differently than adults do. Knowledge of mother tongue acquisition can help the foreign language teacher develop a method which is appropriate to the needs of young learners, according to the following principles:

- Language learning takes place best of all in an anxiety-free and joyful atmosphere.

- The development of receptive skills (listening) takes place before the development of productive skills (speaking).

- Children learn by what they see, hear and do (The parent/child combination of listening, demonstration/movement and visual anchors).

However, the teaching of a foreign language at school requires additional strategies. For one thing, there is a much smaller amount of time for the learning of the foreign language (in comparison to learning to speak one's first language). Therefore the teacher needs to develop methods which allow the child to become a more efficient learner - to receive, process, store and remember information more quickly and effectively.

Insights gained from recent research into the development and workings of the human brain, stress the advantages of a multi-sensory approach to language teaching, based on the following principles:

- When our pupils acquire new information, it comes to them through the senses: they learn from what they see, hear and actually do. The more the individual senses are collectively activated during the reception of new information, the more effectively the pupils will store it (multi-sensory perception).

- When we are processing information, thinking or remembering, our visual, auditory and kinaesthetic (movement) neurological systems are activated. Multi-sensory activation of the brain during these processes increases the pupils' ability to memorise, as well as their concentration and their long-term retention of language information.

- The pupils in a class are normally very different learner types, each favouring this or that sensory channel (with possible weaknesses in the other two sensory channels). Therefore, it is especially important to take the different sensory needs of your learners into consideration. There should be a balance between the visual, auditory and kinaesthetic in all stages of the language teaching process.

- Our memory of vocabulary works associatively. Corresponding forms of presentation, processing and practice are therefore essential for building an effective active vocabulary.

- Stories carry a strong motivation. Through multi-sensory conveyance, these stories (and with them, foreign language information) stay well-anchored in the learner's memory.

- Frequent reconstruction of stories produces a sensitivity toward text grammar in learners. They develop a feel for the inner connections of a text. Thus, ground for the development of productive capability (in the narrative area) is laid.

- Humour, stimulation of pupils' fantasy, vivid illustrations, clear visual aids and a good teaching system are important devices for successful learning.

The basis for the teaching suggestions in **Do and Understand** is James Asher's method TPR (Total Physical Response). TPR is a multi-sensory approach to language teaching, which aims at an intensive training of the learner's receptive capabilities.

Drawing on the latest research into how the brain works, the activities in **Do and Understand** are specifically designed to help the young learner remember new language more efficiently.

3 Teaching with Do and Understand

How you use the stories in **Do and Understand**, will depend, to a certain extent, on the level of your students. With beginners, you may just want to concentrate on using the stories to train your young learners in listening comprehension, following the **Basic techniques** for introducing vocabulary and telling the stories on pages 6 to 10.

Here you will find multi-sensory techniques that will allow you to tell your class a story in a way that they will definitely understand it.

If you want your students to progress to reproducing a story, the **Anchoring Techniques** on pages 10 to 16, give options for working with the stories further, so that they are anchored into the children's long-term memory. You will also find suggestions for working with the worksheets. Using these techniques, the progression from comprehension to reproduction of the stories becomes possible.

With very strong classes, or classes with slightly older children, it is possible to use the stories in **Do and Understand**, as the basis for creative language production. Ideas for such activities are found in the section **Further Application**, on page 16.

3.1 Basic techniques

Preparation for the class

- Select one of the 50 stories, which seems appropriate for the foreign language level of your class, and which you believe will be fun for the children.

- Decide which words and phrases in the story will be new to them.

- Make a simple picture flashcard for each of the new words and phrases (assuming that the words and phrases are ones whose meanings can be portrayed through a drawing). You can use cards made of stiff paper (sized approximately 20cm x 15cm). If you don't have enough time to make cards, you can make sketches on the blackboard or on an overhead for the overhead projector.

- In order to teach the stories to maximum effect, we recommend that you use the picture series or practice worksheets that go with your chosen story (see guidance for using these on page 10, and on pages 15 to 16.) You will need to copy the appropriate number of worksheets for your class.

Setting the context for the stories

Before you teach the story text and vocabulary, you may like to introduce and discuss the content of the story in L1. E.g. with Story 11, *The little mouse*, tell the class that they are going to learn a story about a hungry mouse who likes cheese. Ask pupils (in L1) if any of them have a mouse as a pet, where do mice live, what do they like to eat, etc.

This will increase their interest in the story and make it more meaningful for them. It will also give you an opportunity to discuss any background or cultural points with your pupils (e.g. the things that British people think of as bad luck, as described in story 17).

Introducing vocabulary

It is a good idea to proceed with a multi-sensory introduction of vocabulary. The more the individual senses (visual, auditive and kinaesthetic/motor) are activated during the presentation of the new word, the more successful the introduction of the word's meaning, pronunciation and (written) appearance will be. Furthermore, a multi-sensory approach to new vocabulary guarantees that you will better meet the needs of different learner-types in your class.

The following steps illustrate a tested way of introducing vocabulary, so as to awaken each of the senses.

1   Show your learners the picture flashcards you have prepared, one after another, naming each word as you attach it to the blackboard (with Blue-tack or tape). Or, as you finish each sketch on the board or overhead projector, name the word that is illustrated.

   If the pupils in your class are no longer beginners, it can also be exciting if you don't name the new words right after the presentation of pictures. Try instead to motivate the children to brainstorm words that they associate with the drawings.

2   It is also a good idea, when introducing vocabulary by means of drawings, to anchor each word with a typical hand gesture or with mime. Encourage the pupils to imitate immediately the movements (your miming). Here are some examples for several words in the story, *The little mouse*, on page 19:

You say:	*Simultaneously you make the gesture(s):*
mouse	Run the index and middle finger of your right hand over the upturned palm of your left hand.
look around	Hold your hands like a mouse who's sitting up and begging, and turn your head to the left and right.
hungry	Rub your stomach.
cupboard	First, point at a cupboard in the classroom (to clarify the word's meaning) and then make a square with both hands.

Proceed so that the words are repeated several times. After a while you can leave out the gesture and just say the word. The children should then make the corresponding gesture themselves. In this phase, the children hear the words and/or phrases numerous times and can, therefore, anchor in their memories exactly how they sound.

3   Now present the written form of the words. Hold up the card with the written word and pronounce it simultaneously. In this way, the written version and the oral pronunciation of the word are woven together in the children's memories. Do this with all the words and phrases that are to be introduced.

4   Quickly flash the cards with the words written on them at your learners and get them to shout out the words. The speed of the presentation effectively prevents your class from trying to read the words letter by letter (which often results in faulty pronunciation) and instead facilitates their linking the rough visual representation with what they remember to be the pronunciation. Also, the quick presentation of single words raises their concentration level. When children call out the correct word, you should repeat it and tack the written version next to the appropriate drawing, or you can let a learner tack it up.

Continue the same process with the other words. Another alternative is to flash the card upside down or sideways. Or, instead of presenting the full written word, present a card with just the first letter of the word, which serves as a memory bridge.

5   Then pronounce each of the words again and point to the appropriate pictures. Ask the pupils to close their eyes and listen to you. Pronounce each of the words one more time, loudly and clearly. In this phase, the pupils should not repeat the words after you.

Note If the pupils are not yet used to this way of dealing with vocabulary, they may start giggling when you ask them to close their eyes. An alternative would be to ask them not to close their eyes, but rather to focus their gaze elsewhere, for example, on the ceiling. Many pupils will also want to repeat the words in this phase. Try to explain to them that they should wait a little bit, because really listening to the new words is an important step towards learning to pronounce them.

6   The learners still have their eyes closed. Now say each word aloud and ask the children to repeat each word exactly as you have said it. Vary your voice (whisper, shout, talk in a high pitch, etc.) and get the class to imitate you. The children should also try to visualise the corresponding drawings in their minds.

Note The use of voice variation (loudly, softly, etc.) is an effective memory tool in the auditive area of the brain, just like outlining with coloured pens serves as a memory anchor in the visual area of the brain.

7   "Read my lips."

Ask your pupils to open their eyes again. Mouth one of the words without making any sound. The children should guess which word it is by reading your lips.

Note This simple exercise is very effective because it focuses on each of the sensory channels (visual, kinaesthetic and auditory). The pupils first see you mouthing the word. Unconsciously, they mouth it themselves in order to guess it. Finally, they hear it when it is guessed correctly.

8 What's missing?

Ask the children to close their eyes again. Remove one or more drawings (or cards with the written word) from the board. Ask the children to open their eyes and then find what's missing.

9 Visual anchoring.

Write a number next to each word (drawing + written version) on the board, beginning with the number 1 next to the first word. Tell your learners that they have one minute to concentrate on the numbers and words, and to remember which word goes with which number. After the minute is up, ask them to close their eyes. Say a number and get them to remember the word that goes with it.

This exercise is especially worthwhile because, through its synthetic approach (i.e. overlapping of the various sensory channels), it demonstrates a specific goal-oriented kind of memory training. The visualisation helps to anchor vocabulary in the long-term memory; yet, the other two sensory channels are also associatively involved in the anchoring process. Here, children who have stronger auditory or kinaesthetic channels must practise visualising, too. The ability to visually store written information is a basic key for successful learning at school.

10 Remove all cards and drawings from the board. Ask the children to name the words. Each time a child correctly names a word, he/she should point to the spot on the board where this word was. Write the first letter of this word on the spot.

Another option would be for you to point to a certain spot on the board, after removing all the cards and drawings. The children can now name the word, from memory.

Teaching the stories

Let's assume you have chosen for your lesson the story, *The little mouse* (page 19):

The little mouse
A little mouse comes out of her hole.

She looks around.

The cupboard is open.

She climbs into the cupboard.

There is a plate with cheese on it.

She eats a lot of cheese.

Then she falls asleep.

Dad comes into the kitchen.

He is hungry.

He takes the plate with the cheese on it.

The mouse jumps down.

Dad drops the plate and runs out of the kitchen.

Let's assume you have already worked with the new words and phrases, in the ways mentioned above. The next stage is to get the children to understand the story. The following method is the best way to proceed.

Phase 1

In this phase, you introduce the story using a combination of voice and mime. Pupils imitate your gestures as they hear the story. Ask your learners to stand up and form a circle. (If this isn't possible, they can stand at their usual places.) Tell them that you are going to speak and move at the same time. Ask them to listen, without speaking themselves, and to imitate your movements. Say the first sentence of the story, and as you are saying it, mime its meaning.

You say:	*Simultaneously you mime the following gestures and get the children to imitate your movements:*
A little mouse ...	Make a sign for "little" with your right thumb and index finger.
... comes out ...	Imitate the movements of a mouse with two fingers of your right hand and the upturned palm of your left hand.

... of her hole.	Make a "hole" with your right hand.
She looks around.	Stand like a mouse would stand up on its hind legs (with drawn-up paws) and turn your head left and right, as if you were looking around.
The cupboard is open.	Make a square with your hands, which should symbolise a cupboard, and then make a hand movement which shows that the cupboard is open.
She climbs into the cupboard.	Mime a climbing movement and make a square of the "cupboard" with your hands.

Depending on the performance level of your pupils, it may be a good idea for you to repeat these sentences and their mimed "translation" before you move on to the story's next sentences. Then you can continue:

You say:	**Simultaneously you mime the following gestures and get the children to imitate your movements.**
There's a plate with cheese on it.	Form a "plate" with your upturned hands. Act as if there was a piece of cheese on it. (Smell it, etc.)
She eats a lot of cheese.	Mime eating cheese.
Then she falls asleep.	Close your eyes and drop your head to the side, as if you were falling asleep.

Here again, depending on your group's capability to absorb information, you may want to repeat the sentences and their mimed "translation" before you move on. Then, continue:

Dad comes into the kitchen.	Open an imaginary kitchen door and "walk" (on the spot) into the kitchen.
He is hungry.	Rub your stomach.
He takes the plate with the cheese on it.	With your hand take an imaginary plate.
The mouse jumps down.	Hold up the left palm of your hand. Then lay the fingers of your right hand on top of your left hand. Then make a quick jumping motion to the floor.
Dad drops the plate and runs out of the kitchen.	With a horrified expression on your face, let the "plate" drop and run on the spot.

Repeat the sequence as it is above described as many times as you feel is necessary, depending on your group's level.

Phase 2

In phase 2, children demonstrate their comprehension by performing the gestures by themselves as you tell the story again. In this phase, you do not carry out the movements.

Tell your learners that you will now tell the story again, but that this time, you will not carry out the movements. Now tell the same story (the same sentences as above, in the same order).

You say:

A little mouse comes out of her hole.	The pupils make the gestures.
She looks around.	Etc.

You yourself should not make any movements, but if they gesture correctly, do give positive feedback. (For example, nod.)

Note You will occasionally observe that weaker pupils imitate the better ones in this phase, which is a very natural way of learning for children of this age.

Phase 3

In phase 3, you actively test the children's comprehension by giving the sentences in a jumbled order, for children to mime to. In this way, you will see that they really have grasped the meaning of the sentences and haven't just memorised the mime sequence.

Announce that you are going to say the sentences in a jumbled order, and instruct your learners to carry out the appropriate gestures for each sentence. Now say the sentences that make up the story, but in a different order.

You say:

Dad comes into the kitchen.	The pupils make the appropriate gestures.
The cupboard is open.	Etc.
A little mouse comes out of her hole.	Etc.

Choose individual pupils and give them each a sentence, which they should mime.

Phase 4

Using the picture series worksheets.

Give each learner a copy of the picture series (comic) which illustrates the story. While you read out some of the sentences in jumbled order, your learners should point to the matching picture/s.

Phase 5

Ask your learners to get out a pencil. Say one sentence after another in jumbled order, and before each sentence, a number, starting with number 1. The children should number the pictures accordingly. E.g.

One: There's a plate with cheese on it.

Two: The mouse jumps down.

Three: Dad drops the plate and runs out of the kitchen.

Four: The cupboard is open. Etc.

It is worth working through the worksheet with the children, so that they know if they have numbered the pictures correctly. You could call out each sentence, and they, the appropriate number. This is a good opportunity for you to check how well the children have understood the story.

Note You may find that at first some pupils find it confusing to number the pictures of the story in an order that is different to the narrative sequence. Remember that the point of the exercise is to demonstrate that they really understand each individual sentence of the story, and have not just learnt the narrative sequence by heart. After repeating this type of exercise a couple of times, children should not find it difficult.

However, if you prefer, you could use an alternative method of asking children to mark the pictures, e.g. by using the letters of the alphabet, or colours, instead of numbers.

3.2 Anchoring Techniques

By now, your students will have reached a stage with the story when they understand it completely and have demonstrated this to you by their correct performances of mime and gesture, and by identifying the correct pictures in the picture sequence.

However, it would be a fallacy to assume that learners can immediately reproduce the stories' sentences, even if they have easily understood them. This, however, becomes possible if the stories are practised intensively with the help of anchoring techniques.

We use the term "anchoring" here in the sense that it is used in NLP (Neurolinguistic Programming.) By "anchoring", psychologists understand the often covert process of associating an internal response with some external trigger so that the response may be quickly and effectively reaccessed. Such processing often occurs unconsciously: we hear, for example, a song on the radio and, in the same moment, remember the situation in which we heard this song for the first time. Often we remember with all the senses, that is, we relive old images, voices, conversations, even smells and tastes.

The process of anchoring can be systematically applied in class, in order to aid children in the absorption of foreign language information, as well as to minimise how much they forget. In the coming pages, you will find tested ideas of how you can use visual and kinaesthetic exercises to anchor (auditory) foreign language information in the long-term memory. The suggestions can be used in any order. For each story, you can choose those techniques which you think are best for your actual classroom situation and your learners.

Reconstructing by first letters

Use this exercise only when you believe your learners have understood the story well:

• Demonstrate the first sentence of the story (e.g., *A little mouse comes out of her hole.*) with mime and gesture. Often, a few pupils will already be ready to orally reproduce the sentence or a part of it. Help them to do so, and at the same time, write the sentence on the board, in the form of a skeleton sentence:

A   l   m   c   o   o   h   h.

• Continue in this way until you have written the entire skeleton text on the board.

A	l	m	c	o	o	h	h	.
Sh	l	a	.					
Th	c	i	o	.				
Sh	c	i	th	c	.			
Th	i	a	p	w	ch	o	i	.
Sh	e	a	l	o	ch	.		
Th	sh	f	a	.				
D	c	i	th	k	.			
H	i	h	.					
H	t	th	p	w	th	ch	o	i	.
Th	m	j	d	.				
D	d	th	p	a	r	o	o	th	k	.

- Then you can "read", or rather, reconstruct the text again with your whole class.

- Next, divide the class into pairs and ask them to (orally) reconstruct the text one more time, in their pairs.

- Then erase one letter from each "sentence" on the board. Give the pairs a little time to recall the whole text again, then erase one more letter from each "sentence". Continue erasing until only the first letter of the first word in each sentence remains.

- Reconstructing the entire text will now not be much of a problem for many of your pupils, because they will have internalised the visual anchors on the board (i.e. the letters).

Note The worksheets for stories 1-14 are skeleton texts in the form of first letters and drawings. You can copy them onto overhead transparencies and use them (as described above) by covering the transparency with a sheet of paper and then uncovering the text, line by line. We recommend, however, that you also give your learners a copy of the worksheet and let them "read" it several times. You will notice that many children will be able to reconstruct the story by heart after some time.

Staging the story dramatically - Variation 1

- On a sheet of paper draw a floor plan of the different rooms or spaces, in which your story takes place. On the margin, sketch simple bird's-eye-view drawings of the objects, animals and/or people that appear in the story and that your learners will need to act out the story with as you tell it to them again. (See the following simplified example.)

- Make a copy of the plan for each pupil. Ask your learners to cut out the objects, animals and people. In working with the story *The little mouse*, the children should cut out the drawings of mouse, plate, cheese, Dad, hole, cupboard and door. Now, with the help of the "floor plan", your learners should imagine the space in which the story takes place. Begin by asking your learners to locate particular areas and objects on the "stage".

For example, you say:

Take the mouse hole and put it on the stage.   Walk around the classroom and check whether or not the children have followed your instructions correctly.

Put the door on the stage.   Etc.

- Now, while you read out the story sentence by sentence, the children should move the cut-out paper objects, animals and people and use their hands and fingers to act out the story.

An alternative approach is to use small objects, such as buttons, erasers, pencil sharpeners, etc. to represent the objects, animals and people, instead of paper drawings. In this case, the children should decide what their individual objects represent. (The teacher says, *Show me your mouse*, and each child holds up the corresponding object.)

Staging the story dramatically - Variation 2

For this variation you will need a kind of "Punch and Judy" theatre. You can easily make one yourself with a big cardboard box. In addition, you will need toy figures and various small objects; for our sample story, you'll need a little plastic man *(Dad)*, a mouse, a matchbox *(cupboard)* and an orange pencil sharpener *(cheese)*. Set up the stage so that all the children can see it well.

Ask one or two children to come up to the front and act out the story by moving the toys on the stage, while you read out the story. First, you may want one of the children to introduce each of the objects and what it represents, and to point to the different locations (in this case, the kitchen door, the cupboard, the mouse hole) on the stage. After several repetitions, one or more children might be able to take your place reading out the story.

Scrambled Sentences

- Write the story's sentences on large strips of paper, one sentence per strip.

- Briefly hold up each strip of the story in front of your learners, then hide it from them. As you hide each strip, the children should call out the sentence. (If they call out the sentence after the written version is no longer in sight, interference between the written version and correct pronunciation is avoided.) Repeat this exercise several times.

- Then lay all the paper strips on the floor where all the children can see them. Ask the children to put the jumbled sentences back in the correct order, as they appear in the story.

Variation If you have given your class enough practice in using the skeleton text for text reconstruction, you could write a skeleton version of each sentence as stimulus on the paper strips. Proceed as described above.

Putting the story back in order

- On the left margin of a sheet of paper, sketch the story's drawings in the correct order. Then, on a second sheet of paper, write the story's sentences in a scrambled order. Make copies of both sheets for each pupil.

- The pupils should cut out the scrambled sentences and paste them to the appropriate drawings. (Or you could just hand out the picture sheets and write the sentences on the board or overhead projector. Pupils write the sentences next to the pictures.)

Note Instead of drawing the pictures yourself, you can, of course, photocopy (and reduce the size of) the pictures in this book, and paste them onto the left margin of a sheet of paper.

Puzzle

- Write the story on cards made of stiff paper, with each word in the story on a separate card (sized approximately 20cm x 15cm). The words should be written in on the front of each card in letters big enough to be read by all the children in the class. On the back of each card write the same word that is on the front, but in very small handwriting.

- Attach the cards to the blackboard with the words in the correct order as they appear in the story. The cards should be attached with the hard to read backside showing, so that you can read the small handwriting, but the children can't.

- Now ask your learners to name words in the story. Each time a word is named correctly, turn over the corresponding card, and attach it to the board again, with the front side showing, so that children can read the word. Thus, the entire story will slowly fall into place before the children's very eyes, like a puzzle.

- When the whole story puzzle is complete, ask your learners to close their eyes. Remove one word from every sentence, then get the children to read out the sentences, filling in the blanks from memory. Repeat this process a number of times, each time removing one more word from each sentence, until children are reconstructing the story, from just one word per line.

What's wrong? - Variation 1

Tell your class that you are going to tell the story again. Tell them they should stand up (or knock on their desks, or raise their hands, etc.) whenever they think they've heard you make a mistake. Read out the story again and build in some mistakes, for example:

Teacher:	*A little mouse comes out of her house.*
(Children stand up.)	
Teacher:	*What's wrong?*
Children:	*House!*
Teacher:	*OK. Can you make it right?*
Children:	*A little mouse comes out of her hole.*
Teacher:	*OK. She turns around.*
Etc.	

What's wrong? - Variation 2

Read out a sentence from the story, but carry out the physical gestures that belong to a different sentence. The pupils should correct you, either by making the correct gestures, or by calling out the sentence that corresponds to your mime.

Memory - Variation 1

Photocopy the picture story worksheet that goes with your story, and cut out the individual pictures. You will need two sets of pictures per group of four children. (Your learners can help you with the cutting out of the pictures.)

The learners work in groups of four. Each group shuffles the pictures and lays them out in front of them, face down, on the floor or on a table. The object of the game is to find the matching pairs. One child begins by picking up one card. This child must say the sentence that corresponds to the card. Then he/she should draw another card, and again, name the corresponding sentence. If the two pictures match, the child can keep both cards. If not, it's the next child's turn.

Memory - Variation 2

Photocopy the picture story worksheet that goes with your story, and cut out the individual pictures. You will need one sheet per pupil in the class.

Each child lays all the cut-out pictures from the picture story in front of him/her. You read out one sentence from the story. Whoever holds up the correct picture first, wins a point. (This can also be played in teams.)

Variation for a more advanced class: whoever holds up the correct picture first, gets to say the next sentence.

Memory - Variation 3

Call up one pupil to the front of the class. Tell him/her three or four sentences from the story in any order. The pupil should listen with concentration, and then act out the sentences. (Depending on the class level you can give more or fewer sentences.)

Note Give your learners a hint: this exercise is easier to do, if while they are listening, they imagine the sentences are a comic strip, and then later, they can imitate the action of this comic strip.

Show me the picture

Photocopy the picture story worksheet that goes with your story, and cut out the individual pictures. Give each child in the class one picture. If you have more pupils than pictures, then cut up a second copy of the worksheet and distribute these pictures, too. If you have too few pupils, give some children a second, or if necessary, a third picture.

Ask the children to hold up their picture whenever they hear the sentence to which it belongs. Now read the story sentence by sentence and check to see if the pictures that the children hold up match the sentences you've read. If no one holds up a picture, or if a child holds up the wrong picture, read the sentence again, and again, until someone shows you the correct picture.

Show me the action

Change the story's sentences slightly by adding in words that your class has learned in earlier lessons. The following example comes from a school lesson, in which the teacher and children had worked on the story *The little mouse*. This teacher gave her pupils the following instructions:

Teacher: *Who can do this? The mouse comes out of a schoolbag.* (The children laugh.) *Sandra?*

(Sandra, the chosen pupil, acts out the new sentence.)

Good, Sandra.

Next sentence. Dad comes into the kitchen. He falls asleep. Who can do it?
(Several children raise their hands.)
OK. Tom, please.
Etc.

Which new instructions you can give your learners depend greatly upon their current knowledge of English. For the learners, acting out the new sentences is a lot of fun, because their content is mostly unexpected and surprising. It can also be an important affirmation of individual listening comprehension performance, if a child is able to understand and act out a sentence that he/she has never heard before.

Using the practice worksheets in Do and Understand

For every picture story, there is also a practice worksheet. The practice worksheets vary in activity type and their purpose is to help anchor the stories in young learners' long-term memories. We recommend using the practice worksheets in the following ways:

Worksheets 1-14, 46 (See also: Reconstructing by first letters)

The pupils construct the story from their memories. The first letters and drawings help guide them. In advanced classes, in which the pupils already know how to write in the foreign language, the worksheets can also serve as memory bridges while writing the text.

To help pupils check their own language accuracy, the complete story text should later be displayed, for children to compare with their own version, which they can correct as necessary. The story text can be displayed with the help of an overhead projector; or copies of the text can be hung up on the classroom walls.

Worksheets 15-20 (See also: Putting the story back in order)

These can be used in a variety of ways:

- The children cut out the jumbled sentences and paste them to the matching pictures.

- The children search for the sentence that goes with the picture. Then they write the sentence next to the picture.

- The children match the pictures to the sentences by numbering both.

Worksheet 21

The children look at the pictures and then write the correct numbers in the boxes in front of the appropriate sentences.

Worksheets 22, 37

The children mark the sentence that goes with the picture.

Worksheets 23, 28, 42

The children separate the individual sentences by colouring them with different coloured pens or pencils.

Worksheets 24, 34

The children connect sentence-halves by underlining them or circling them with the same coloured pen. They could also cut out the sentence-halves and paste them to a prepared worksheet.

Worksheets 25, 35, 39

These exercises are more meaningful if the children have first seen the entire text. Give your learners one hint: to cross out each letter in the box after they have used it.

Worksheets 26, 36, 38, 45

Again, tell your learners to cross out each word in the box after they have used it.The children write the correct number on the picture.

Worksheets 27, 29, 32, 40

The children read the story and write numbers by the appropriate pictures or words. Here, it is important that they do not have access to the picture stories.

Worksheet 30

After the children have written numbers in the boxes, they should take another look at the picture story (as a corrective measure). Only then should they read out their results.

Worksheet 31

The children mark the correct pictures.

Worksheet 33

The children mark the correct words and phrases.

Worksheets 41, 49

First the children number the words in the correct order, then they write down the sentences.

Worksheets 43, 44

The children replace the wrong words, then they write the story.

Worksheets 47, 50

The children look for sentence parts that belong together. Then they write the story.

Worksheet 48

First the children underline the correct answer in each box, then they write the story.

3.3 Further application of Do and Understand

From reproduction to production

Once you have intensively practised a story with your learners, and once they are familiar with the basic routines of anchoring, you may ask them to give the commands in your place. These commands can then be acted out by the whole class or by just a few pupils. This role reversal should be welcomed, but by no means demanded too early from the learners. In other words, you should wait for learners to volunteer.

As far as pronunciation mistakes and other mistakes are concerned, we suggest that you do not interrupt the children while they are talking. (Or if you do, whisper the correction.) It is better to wait until the child is finished and then correct mistakes later (for example, by drilling a sentence with the entire class). James Asher warns:

> "Remember, their entire attention is directed to the monumental task of production. They do not have attention units available to process feedback from you. Any early demand for perfection in speech will tend to inhibit production. Let them talk and talk and talk. Eventually, they can be fine-tuned for more perfection."

(From *Learning Another Language Through Action,* 1988.)

Encouraging creative production: a model

After some time (how long depends on the level of your class) you will find it possible to challenge your pupils to come up with creative ideas as to how the model texts could be changed. This could first be done as a class task, with the teacher facilitating the process. The basic procedure is as follows:

- Write the skeleton text on the board.

- Erase those letters that stand for words that could easily be replaced by other words. For example, in our sample skeleton text, *The little mouse*, you could erase *m* for *mouse* from the first sentence.

- Ask your learners to suggest words that could replace mouse. If the children do not know the proper word and you speak their mother tongue, you should get them to ask you for the English word with the following phrase: What's . . . in English?

- Say the new English word, and at the same time, write its first letter in the place of the letter you have just erased.

- Continue this process with the rest of the model text.

Get the pupils to think about which changes in the text would be possible or meaningful. The following example was produced by a class of nine-year-olds, with the help of their teacher:

The little spider

A little spider comes out of its web.
It looks at the table.
There is some chocolate on it.
The spider climbs onto the table.
It eats a lot of chocolate.
Then it dances.
Mum comes into the kitchen.
She wants to eat some chocolate.
She takes the chocolate.
She sees the spider.
Mum drops the chocolate and runs out of the kitchen.

4 Authors' acknowledgements

First of all we would like to thank Prof. James Asher, who developed the Total Physical Response (TPR) method. We have found TPR extremely stimulating and helpful when teaching young learners. We would also like to thank the children of our trial classes and their teachers, who piloted our ideas with great enthusiasm. Thanks are also due to Monika Siglreithmaier (*Feeding squirrels*), Elisabeth Skopal and Theresia Zils (*Eating spaghetti*), Eva Salem and Brigitte Hainthaler (*The little mouse*), Karin Hansal, Elisabeth Schneider and Elfriede Molik (*The roses*), Elfriede Sayfried (*The little cat*) as well as to the members of the AG Steiermark (*Dad's shoes*, *A mistake* and *The snowman*).

The publishers wish to apologise for the misleading text in these Acknowledgements in the first impression of this edition, relating to James Asher.

5 Suggested reading

James Asher, *Learning Another Language Through Action*, Sky Oaks Publications, Los Gatos, 1988.

James Asher, *Brainswitching. A Skill for the 21st Century,* Sky Oaks Publications, Los Gatos, 1988.

Michael Grinder, *Righting the Educational Conveyor Belt*, Metamorphous Press, 1989.

Story Texts

The following are the complete texts for the fifty action stories. The texts correspond to the picture story and activity worksheets on pages 26 to 125. Select a text which you think is appropriate for your learners' language level, and which they will enjoy.

Before teaching the story, you may want to discuss the context for it in L1, either to arouse the children's interest in the story they are going to hear, or to discuss any background information you think will be necessary. For example, for story 17, *Bad luck*, begin the class by discussing things that are considered bad luck in the country you are in. Then you can tell learners how this compares to things that are considered bad luck in Britain.

Story 1 • Off to school

Turn off the alarm clock.
Get out of bed.
Put on your jeans and your T-shirt.
Have a glass of milk.
Get your schoolbag.
Run to the bus stop.
Look at your feet.
You've got your slippers on.
Shout, "Oh no!"

Story 2 • The butterfly

Take a piece of paper and a pencil.
Draw a butterfly.
Get your paints.
Colour the butterfly.
Cut out the butterfly.
Carry it to the window.
Open the window.
Blow softly on the butterfly.
Watch it fly away.

Story 3 • Sun tan

It's a hot day.
Go to the beach.
Put sun lotion on your face, arms, legs, back and chest.
Put your towel on the sand and lie down.
You go to sleep.
You wake up.
Touch your arms, your legs, your back and your face.
They hurt.
Say, "Stupid me!"

Story 4 • The little cat

A little cat is sitting next to a window.
She looks into the garden.
Suddenly she can hear a bird.
The bird is on the garden table.
It's eating some cake on a plate.
The cat is hungry.
She jumps down.
Crash. The plate breaks.
Now the bird is sitting in a tree.

Story 5 • Dad's shoes

Dad is looking for his shoes.
He looks under the bed.
He looks behind the curtains.
He looks in the cupboard.
He looks in the bathroom.
You are in front of the washing machine.
Open the washing machine.
Take out Dad's shoes.
"Here they are," you say, "they are clean now."

Story 6 • Phone box

You want to make a phone call.
Look for a phone box.
A man is in the phone box.
Wait for five minutes.
The man is still talking.
Open the door.
Say, "Excuse me, your car is on fire."
The man runs away.
You make your phone call.

Story 7 • The snowman

It's snowing.
Make a big snowman.
Take a pot.
Put it on the snowman's head.
Take two buttons.
Stick them into the snowman's head.
Take a big carrot.
Stick it into the snowman's head.

There is a rabbit in the garden.
It looks very hungry.
The snowman is scared.
He runs away.

Story 8 • Looking for mushrooms

Take a basket.
Go into the woods.
Look for mushrooms.
You can see a little rabbit.
It runs away.
Follow the little rabbit.
It hides in the bushes.
Oh! You can see a big mushroom.
Pick the mushroom and put it in your
    basket.
Walk home.
Cut the mushroom.
Cook it.
Eat it.
Mmmh, it tastes good.
Say, "Thank you, little rabbit."

Story 9 • The watch

You've lost your watch.
You look in your schoolbag. Nothing.
You look in your desk. Nothing.
You look under your desk. Nothing.
You look under the carpet. Nothing.
You look behind the TV. Nothing.
You look under the bed. Nothing.
You look behind the piano. Nothing.
Your dog comes into your room.
He is wagging his tail.
What has he got in his mouth?
It's your watch.

Story 10 • The roses

Look out of the window.
The sun is shining.
Go into the garden.
Smell the beautiful roses.
You have an idea.
Get some scissors.
Cut twenty beautiful roses.
Run into the house.
Shout, "Mum, mum."
Give the roses to your mother.
Your mother has tears in her eyes.
She is so happy.

Story 11 • The little mouse

A little mouse comes out of her hole.
She looks around.
The cupboard is open.
She climbs into the cupboard.
There is a plate with cheese on it.
She eats a lot of cheese.
Then she falls asleep.
Dad comes into the kitchen.
He is hungry.
He takes the plate with the cheese on
    it.
The mouse jumps down.
Dad drops the plate and runs out of the
    kitchen.

Story 12 • The banana

Go to a shop.
Buy a banana.
Peel it.
Eat the banana.
Throw the peel on the ground.
A woman is leaving the shop.
She slips on the peel and falls.
Help the woman.
Pick up her bag.
The woman gives you 50p.
Say "Thank you" and put the 50p in
    your pocket.
You slip on the banana peel.

Story 13 The fence

It's a lovely day.
You are walking through a field.
You come to a fence.
Climb over the fence.
Suddenly you hear a noise.
You turn round.
There's a big bull in front of you.
The bull looks at you.
Say "I'm sorry."
Slowly walk backwards until you come
    to the fence again.
Climb over the fence.
Wipe your forehead.

Story 14 • The fly

Dad is sitting in front of the television.
He is watching a football match.
A fly is circling his head.
The fly lands on his head.
Take a newspaper.

Quietly put a chair next to your dad's
    chair.
Climb on it.
Hit dad's head with the newspaper.
Dad screams and jumps up.
Say "Sorry."
Point at the fly.
It is circling the television.

Story 15 • Feeding squirrels

Fill a bag with nuts
Go to the park.
Sit down on a bench.
Feed the squirrels.
The wind starts blowing.
You feel cold.
Run home.
Put the kettle on.
Have a cup of tea.
Have a big sandwich.
There is a knock at the window.
You look up. It's a hungry squirrel.

Story 16 • On the bus

Get on a bus.
Buy a ticket.
Sit down.
You feel hungry.
Look for food in your pockets.
Nothing.
Put the ticket in your mouth
Chew it.
The inspector comes and wants to see
    your ticket.
Take the ticket out of your mouth.
Show it to the inspector.
The inspector is very angry.

Story 17 • Bad luck

It's a Friday morning.
You get out of bed on the wrong side.
You see a black spider in one corner of
    your room.
In the bathroom you break a mirror.
At breakfast you burn your tongue.
On your way to school a black cat
    crosses your way.
Then you walk under a ladder.
In the maths lesson the teacher gives
    back the tests.
You are scared.
Your hands shake.

You open your testbook.
It says "Excellent."

Story 18 • The windmill

Take a big, square piece of paper.
Take a long stick and a pin.
Fold the edges of the paper to the
    middle.
Fix the paper with the pin on the stick.
Colour your windmill.
Take some sellotape.
Fix the windmill on your bike.
Get on your bike.
Ride it fast.
The windmill goes, "z-z-z-z-z-z-z-z-z".
Your bike takes off.
You fly up into the sky.

Story 19 • A mistake

You wake up.
Jump out of your bed.
Stretch your arms.
Go into the bathroom.
Wash your face.
Clean your teeth.
Put on your clothes.
Look for your schoolbag.
Suddenly you remember.
Take off your clothes.
Jump back into bed.
It's the first day of the holidays.

Story 20 A bad day

You get out of bed.
You fall over your schoolbag. Aaah.
Put on your shirt.
A button is missing.
Get a needle and thread from the
    kitchen.
You bump into the table. Ouch.
Sew on the button.
You prick your finger. Ouch.
Get a plaster from the bathroom.
You fall over a chair. Ouch.
Shout.
Go back to bed.

Story 21 • Going fishing

Take your fishing rod.
Walk down to the river.
Throw out the line.
There's a sharp pull.

Roll in the line.
There's a big fish on it.
Make a fire.
Cook the fish.
You hear a dog howl.
Start eating.
Look up. The dog is sitting opposite
  you.
Throw the dog a piece of fish.

Story 22 • The birthday party

You go to a birthday party.
Give your present to your friend.
Have some orange juice.
Have a piece of cake.
Clap your hands to the music.
Ask a girl to dance with you.
Start dancing.
You fall and hurt your leg.
The girl helps you up.
Sit down on a chair.
Hold your leg.
The girl pats your cheek and you
  blush.

Story 23 • Going for a walk

The sun is shining. It is a beautiful day.
Go for a walk.
What's that? You can hear a roll of
  thunder.
There are big black clouds in the sky.
It starts pouring down.
Run home.
Your hair gets wet.
Your face gets wet.
Your neck gets wet.
Your shirt gets wet.
Your jeans get wet.
Your shoes get wet.
Yuck!

Story 24 • Bow and arrow

Say hello to your neighbours.
They are having tea in their garden.
Take out your pocket knife.
Cut a stick from the bush in your
  garden.
Take a piece of string.
Make a bow.
Cut a small stick from the bush.
Make an arrow.
Put it on the string.

Shoot it high up in the sky.
The arrow comes down.
It lands in your neighbours' chocolate
  cake.

Story 25 • Swapping

You hear the postman.
Run to the letter box.
There is a letter for your mother.
Take the letter to your mother.
She opens the envelope and puts it on
  the table.
Take the scissors and cut out the
  stamps.
Put the stamps in your schoolbag.
Leave for school.
It's lunchtime. Get out your sandwich.
Your friend has got a big apple.
Swap the stamps for the apple.
Eat the apple.

Story 26 • Going shopping

Your mother gives you a shopping list.
Take a basket.
Get your bike from the garage.
Jump on it.
One pedal comes off.
Get your brother's bike.
It has got a flat tyre.
Walk to the shop.
Buy all the things on your list.
Carry them home.
You are hot.
Your mother gives you a big bowl of ice
  cream. Yummy.

Story 27 • The new girl

There is a new girl with her dog in the
  park.
She has got brown eyes and a pony
  tail.
You walk on your hands.
The girl looks at you, but she doesn't
  smile.
Run over to the sweet shop.
Buy a lolly.
Walk over to the girl.
There is another boy next to her.
He is giving her an ice cream.
She takes the ice cream and begins to
  eat it.
She smiles at the other boy.

Give the lolly to the girl's dog.

Story 28 • Going by plane

Say good-bye to your friends.
Put your bag in the X-ray machine.
Pick up your bag.
Show your boarding pass.
Get on the plane.
Put your bag in the overhead locker.
Sit down and put the seat belt on.
Lean back.
Smile. In three hours' time you'll be
  home.

Story 29 • Your sister

You are going to bed.
Your sister is in the bathroom.
Go into the kitchen.
Open the fridge.
Take out some ice.
Take the ice to your sister's room.
Put the ice under the cover.
Go into your room and listen at the
  door.
A minute passes.
You can hear your sister scream.
Jump into bed.
Switch off the light and close your eyes.

Story 30 • Mineral water

Your family are having dinner.
You are thirsty.
The bottle of mineral water is empty.
Stand up.
Go into the kitchen.
Take a bottle from the fridge.
Rock the bottle like a baby.
Put the bottle on the table.
Unscrew it.
Whoosh.
Wipe your face.
Fill all the glasses.

Story 31 • The mask

Get a piece of paper.
Get some colour pencils.
Draw a head.
Draw a big nose with warts.
Draw an ugly mouth with big teeth.
Make two holes for eyes.
Cut out the head.
Hold it in front of your face.

Creep into your mum and dad's
  bedroom.
Shout "Argh..."
Your mum and dad look very white.
Get your mum and dad a cup of coffee.

Story 32 • Going to a fancy dress party

Go into the bathroom.
Stand in front of the mirror.
Take some lipstick.
Put it on.
Take a black pencil.
Draw black circles round your eyes.
Put your Dracula teeth in your mouth.
Put green colour on your hair.
Your mother comes into the bathroom.
She screams.
You want to kiss her.
She runs out of the bathroom.

Story 33 • The bird

Your teacher tells you to write a story.
You look out of the window.
You can see a bird on a tree.
Suddenly you hear the bang of a gun.
The bird falls down on the ground.
A man with a gun picks up the bird.
You feel angry and sad.
You start writing your story.
It's about a man.
He aims his gun at a bird.
A big ant sees this and bites the man's
  leg.
The man says "Ouch!" and the bird
  flies away.

Story 34 • Grandpa

You knock at grandpa's door.
You listen. Nothing.
You open the door. No grandpa there.
Grandpa's glasses are on the table.
The newspaper is on the chair.
You look around.
You hear a strange noise.
Monsters! Monsters have kidnapped
  your grandpa.
You run into the kitchen.
Father comes back with you.
You can hear the strange noise again
  from behind the curtains.
You open the curtains. There is grandpa.

Story 35 • In a hurry

Look at your watch.
You are in a hurry.
Run to the bus stop.
You see some stickers in a shop window.
Go into the shop and pick up the
  stickers.
You see a man talking to the shop
  assistant.
Stare at the man's neck.
The man puts his hands on his neck
  and stops talking.
Pay for the stickers.
Stare at the man's neck again and wink
  twice.
The man looks confused.
Smile at him and say goodbye.

Story 36 • The Man in the Moon

You are asleep in your bed.
The moon is shining through your
  window.
Suddenly the Man in the Moon is in your
  room.
He takes your hand.
You put on your jeans and T-shirt.
You get into a spaceship.
He takes you to the moon.
There are lots of people.
They are dancing rock 'n' roll.
You dance with them.
Suddenly you hear a noise.
You listen.
It's the alarm clock.
You get out of bed.
You are wearing your jeans and T-shirt.

Story 37 • At the seaside

A boy is looking at the sea.
His friends are swimming and playing
  with a ball.
He is scared of the sea.
Suddenly the boy can see a dark
  shadow.
It's a dolphin.
It jumps out of the water.
It smiles at the boy.
The boy runs into the water.
He holds on to the dolphin's fin.
He glides through the water with the
  dolphin.
Then the dolphin brings him back to
the beach.
The boy waves goodbye.

Story 38 • Chasing wasps

Get a glass of orange juice.
Sit down at the table in the garden.
Drink the orange juice.
A wasp flies into the glass.
Pick up a newspaper.
Stand up and chase the wasp away.
Two wasps circle your head.
Chase them away.
Ten wasps attack you.
Put the glass on the table.
Shout "Aaah!"
Run away.

Story 39 • The treasure

One night you dream of treasure.
The next day you get into your boat.
You row to an island.
You take your spade and walk to a
  tree.
You begin to dig.
After three hours you feel very tired.
You lie down and go to sleep.
You have another dream.
The treasure is in your mother's oven.
You run to your boat and row home.
At home you look into the oven.
There is your treasure. Roast chicken.
Yummy.

Story 40 The Picnic

Take a basket.
Put in a blanket.
Put in some cheese, some bread,
  some butter, some orange juice and
  a knife.
Take your bike and go to the
  countryside.
Stop.
Take out the blanket and sit down.
Eat and drink. Yummy. It's wonderful.
You are tired.
You fall asleep.
You dream of a beautiful lake.
There is a big fish in the lake.
It splashes water at you.
Your face gets wet.
You open your eyes.
It's raining.

Story 41 • Making breakfast

You are at home alone.
You are very hungry.
You take some milk from the fridge.
Drink. Mmh.
You find some cornflakes.
Eat some cornflakes. Yummy.
Take a big bowl.
Pour milk and cornflakes into the bowl.
Get an apple, a banana, a pear and a
  peach.
Cut up the fruit.
Taste a bit of everything.
Put the fruit into the bowl.
Get a spoon.
Sit down to eat.
You don't feel hungry now.
Pick up the bowl and put it in the
  fridge.

Story 42 • Down the river

You are paddling down a river in the
  jungle.
You are tired.
Paddle to the river bank.
Pull your boat on the bank.
Take off your jeans and shoes.
Sit down on a log.
The log starts to move.
It's a crocodile.
Run into the jungle.
Climb a tree.
There is a big snake hanging from a
  branch.
Climb down.
Rest.
Suddenly you can hear a jaguar roar.
Run back to your boat and jump in.
Paddle away.

Story 43 • The young magician

The old magician leaves the castle.
The young magician opens the
  cupboard.
He takes out a big book.
He opens the book and begins to read.
Then he gets a plate.
He reads aloud from the book.
Suddenly there is a wonderful pink
  cake on the plate.
When he touches it, the cake gets
  smaller and smaller.

The young magician shouts, "Stop".
But the cake is very small now.
Then the old magician comes home.
He starts laughing.
Then he says some magic words.
The cake gets bigger again.
The boy and the old man sit down and
  eat it.

Story 44 Eating spaghetti

Go to a restaurant.
Sit down at a table.
Call the waiter and order spaghetti.
The waiter brings the spaghetti.
He falls and drops the spaghetti.
Wipe the spaghetti off your trousers.
The waiter brings another plate of
  spaghetti.
Start eating.
There's spaghetti on the table.
There's spaghetti on the floor.
But there's no spaghetti in your mouth.
Call the waiter and ask for a knife.
The waiter brings you a knife.
Cut the spaghetti.
Eat it with your spoon.
Wonderful spaghetti.

Story 45 • Maths homework

Open your maths book.
Try to concentrate.
Get a sharpener.
Sharpen a pencil.
You feel hungry.
Get a sandwich from the kitchen.
Look again at your maths homework.
Put a cassette into your cassette
  recorder.
Listen to the cassette.
You feel thirsty.
Get a glass of milk from the kitchen.
Switch on the TV.
Watch TV.
Listen. You can hear your dad.
Switch off the TV.
Say "Dad, help me with my maths
  homework, please."

Story 46 • Little green men

Go for a walk in the woods.
You come to a field.
You see a spaceship!

Walk to the spaceship.
The door of the spaceship opens.
Two little green men look out.
They are wearing big helmets.
They invite you in.
You sit down.
They give you something to drink.
It tastes wonderful.
Stand up and say goodbye.
Run home.
Your mum says, "Where were you?"
You say, "I was in a spaceship with two
little green men."
Your mum says, "Don't be silly!"

Story 47 • The balloon

Your dad gives you a balloon.
Take a sheet of paper.
Write a little story.
Get your photo and stick it on the
paper.
Take a piece of string.
Tie the paper to the balloon.
Go out into the street.
Let the balloon go.
The balloon is flying higher and higher.
In another town a boy sees the
balloon.
The balloon comes down.
He takes the paper and unfolds it.
He looks at the picture.
He likes the story and the photo.
But he looks sad because there is no
address.

Story 48 • Chasing a monster

It's a Sunday morning.
Your parents are asleep.
You feel hungry.
Go into the kitchen.
There's a monster sitting at the table
eating cornflakes.
The monster is brown.
It has yellow eyes, blue fingernails and
orange teeth.
Take the cornflakes away.
Shout "Get out."
The monster jumps up and runs
upstairs.
You run after the monster.
You can hear your parents scream.
You look into their bedroom.

The window is open.
Look out of the window.
You can see the monster eating your
dad's car.
Shout. "Stop! You can have some
cornflakes."

Story 49 • Superboy

Superboy is walking in a wood.
He walks to a pool.
He sees a girl. She is crying.
She is looking into the water.
Superboy looks into the water.
He can see a golden crown.
Superboy dives into the water.
He picks up the crown.
Then he swims to the girl.
He gives her the crown.
The girl kisses Superboy.
There is a loud noise. Boom.
Superboy changes into a horse.
The girl gets on the horse and rides
away.

Story 50 • Treasure hunt

You are reading in a very old book.
You find a very old piece of paper with a
drawing in your book.
It's a treasure map.
The treasure is in a castle on a small
island in the sea.
Take an atlas and look for the small
island.
Take your bike and ride to the sea.
Get into a boat.
Row to the island.
Get out of the boat.
The castle is on top of a big hill.
Open the castle's big gate.
Go down into the cellar.
There is a box.
Open it.
There's a piece of paper in it.
It says, "Well done".

Do and Understand – © This edition Addison Wesley Longman Limited 1996

OFF TO SCHOOL

Read the story.

T   o   t   .

G   o   of   .

P   o   y   and y   .

H   a   of   .

G   y   .

to   th   .

L   at   y   f   .

You've   g   y   o   .

S   , "Oh   n !"

The butterfly

Do and Understand – © This edition Addison Wesley Longman Limited 1996

Read the story.

SUN TAN

Read the story.

It's a h d .

Go t th .

P ☀ l o y 👤, 🦵, 🦵 a 👕.

P y 🧴 o th s and l d .

Y g t s .

Y w u .

T y 🦾 , y 🦵 ,y 👤 and y 👤.

Th h .

S , "S n m !"

THE LITTLE CAT

Do and Understand – © This edition Addison Wesley Longman Limited 1996

THE LITTLE CAT

Read the story.

A l 🐱 is sitting next to a 🪟

S 🐱 into the 🌳.

S s c 🐱 a 🐦.

T 🐦 i o t 🌳 🪑.

It's 🐦 some 🍰 on a 🍽 .

T 🐱 is h .

S 🐱 .

C . T 🍽 b .

N t 🐦 i s i a 🌳.

Dad's shoes

Here they are.

Do and Understand – © This edition Addison Wesley Longman Limited 1996

Read the story.

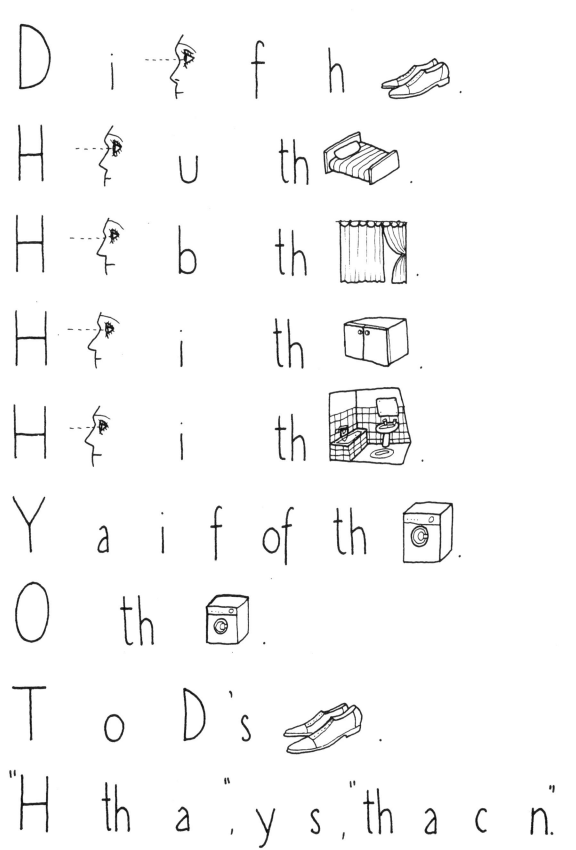

Phone box

Do and Understand – © This edition Addison Wesley Longman Limited 1996

Phone box

Read the story.

Y w to m a p c .

 f a .

A i in th .

W f 5 m .

Th i s t .

O th .

S , "E m , y i o ."

Th r a .

Y m y p c .

STORY 7

The snowman

Read the story.

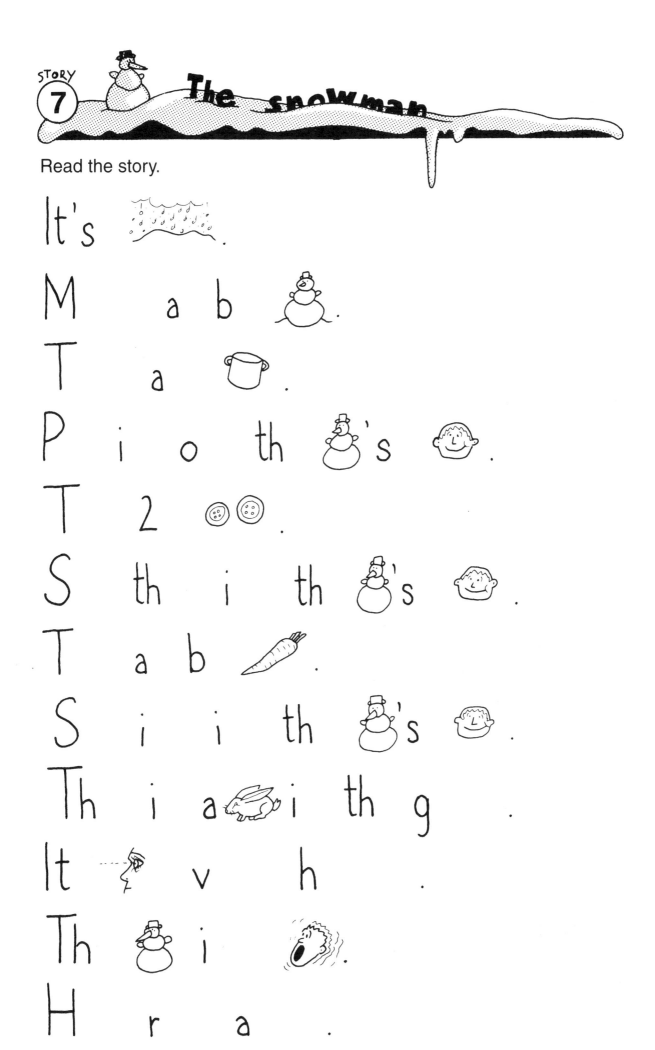

It's  .

M a b  .

T a  .

P i o th  's  .

T 2 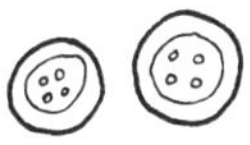 .

S th i th  's  .

T a b  .

S i i th  's  .

Th i a  i th g .

It  v h .

Th  i  .

H r a .

Looking for mushrooms

Do and Understand – © This edition Addison Wesley Longman Limited 1996

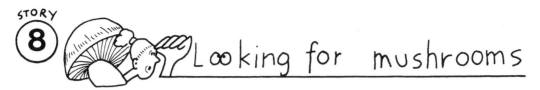 Looking for mushrooms

Read the story.

T   a 🧺 .

G   i   th 🌳 .

L for 🍄 .

Y c 👁 a l 🐰

I r   a .

F th l 🐰 .

I h in t 🌿 .

Oh! Y c 👁 a b 🍄 .

P th 🍄 a p it in y 🧺 .

W h .

C th 🍄 .

C it .

🧒 it .

Mmmh, it t g .

S "Th y , l 🐰 ".

Read the story.

You've l y .

Y Y i y . N .

Y Y i y . N .

Y Y u y . N .

Y Y u th . N .

Y Y b th . N .

Y Y u th . N .

Y Y b th . N .

Y c i y r .

H i w h .

W h h g in h ?

It's y .

Do and Understand – © This edition Addison Wesley Longman Limited 1996

The roses

Do and Understand – © This edition Addison Wesley Longman Limited 1996

The roses

Read the story.

Do and Understand – © This edition Addison Wesley Longman Limited 1996

the little mouse

Read the story.

A l  c o of h  .

S  a .

Th  i o .

S c i th  .

Th . i a  w  o it .

S e a l o  .

Th s f a .

D c i th k .

H i h .

H t th  w th  o it .

Th   .

D  t  a r o of th k .

The banana

Do and Understand – © This edition Addison Wesley Longman Limited 1996

The banana

Read the story.

G t a  .

B a  .

P i .

E th  .

Thr th p o th  .

A  i l th  .

Sh  o th p a  .

H th  .

P u h  .

Th  g y  .

S "Th y" a p th  i y  .

Y  o th b p .

Do and Understand – © This edition Addison Wesley Longman Limited 1996

STORY 13

The fence

Read the story.

It's a l d

Y a w thr a .

Y c t a .

 o th f .

S y  a n .

Y .

Th 's a b  i f of y .

Th   a y .

S , "I'm s ."

S . u y. c t th  a .

 o th .

W y .

STORY 14 The fly

Do and Understand – © This edition Addison Wesley Longman Limited 1996

The fly

Read the story.

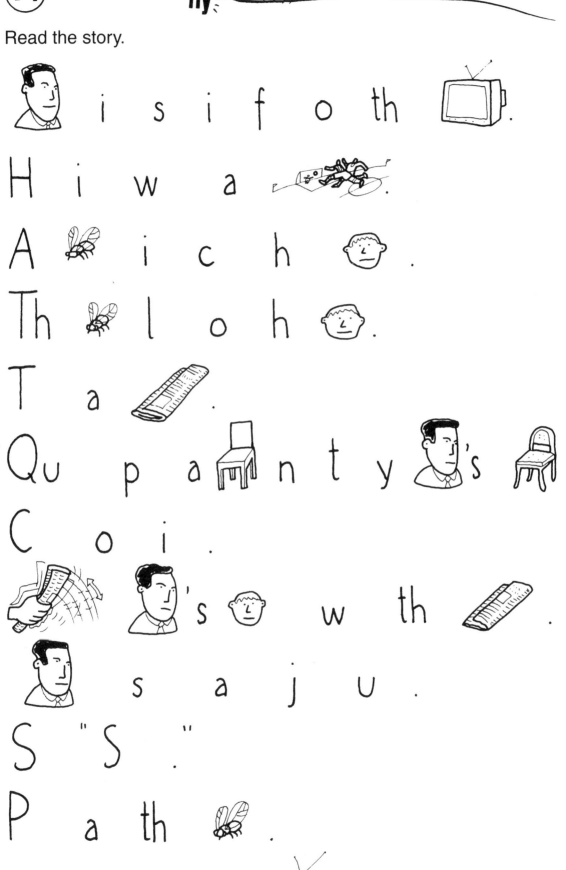

STORY 15 FEEDING SQUIRRELS

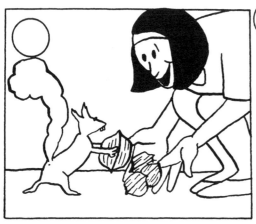
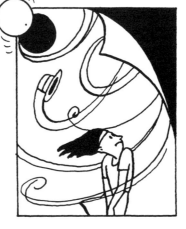

Do and Understand – © This edition Addison Wesley Longman Limited 1996

FEEDING SQUIRRELS

Match the pictures with the sentences.

Fill a bag with nuts.	Run home.	The wind starts blowing.
Feed the squirrels.	Go to the park.	
You feel cold.	Sit down on a bench.	Have a big sandwich.
You look up. It's a hungry squirrel.	There is a knock at the window.	Put the kettle on.
		Have a cup of tea.

55

Do and Understand – © This edition Addison Wesley Longman Limited 1996

ON THE BUS

Match the pictures with the sentences.

The inspector comes and wants to see your ticket.	Look for food in your pockets.	The inspector is very angry.
You feel hungry.	Take the ticket out of your mouth.	Put the ticket in your mouth.
Get on a bus.	Nothing.	Sit down.
Show it to the inspector.	Chew it.	Buy a ticket.

Do and Understand – © This edition Addison Wesley Longman Limited 1996

bad luck

Do and Understand – © This edition Addison Wesley Longman Limited 1996

Bad luck

Match the pictures with the sentences.

You open your testbook.	You see a black spider in one corner of your room.	In the maths lesson the teacher gives back the tests.
You get out of bed on the wrong side.	It says, "Excellent."	On your way to school a black cat crosses your way.
Then you walk under a ladder.	Your hands shake.	
You are scared.	In the bathroom you break a mirror.	At breakfast you burn your tongue.
It's a Friday morning.		

The windmill

Do and Understand – © This edition Addison Wesley Longman Limited 1996

STORY **18**  The windmill

Match the pictures with the sentences.

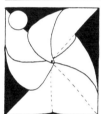

Colour your windmill.	Fold the edges of the paper to the middle.	The windmill goes, "z-z-z-z-z-z-z-z-z-z".
Get on your bike.		
You fly up into the sky.	Fix the windmill on your bike.	Take a long stick and a pin.
Take a big, square piece of paper.	Fix the paper with the pin on the stick.	Ride it fast.
Your bike takes off.		Take some sellotape.

A MISTAKE

  A MISTAKE

Match the pictures with the sentences.

Go into the bathroom.	Jump back into bed.	Take off your clothes.
Jump out of your bed.	Suddenly you remember.	Wash your face.
It's the first day of the holidays.		Look for your schoolbag.
	Stretch your arms.	
Put on your clothes.	You wake up.	Clean your teeth.

Do and Understand – © This edition Addison Wesley Longman Limited 1996

Do and Understand – © This edition Addison Wesley Longman Limited 1996

Match the pictures with the sentences.

Go back to bed.	A button is missing.	You prick your finger. Ouch.
You bump into the table. Ouch.	You fall over your schoolbag. Aaah.	Get a needle and thread from the kitchen.
Put on your shirt.	You fall over a chair. Ouch.	Get a plaster from the bathroom.
Shout.	Sew on the button.	
You get out of bed.		

GOING FISHING

Do and Understand – © This edition Addison Wesley Longman Limited 1996

GOING FISHING

Write the numbers in the boxes.

- [ ] Start eating.
- [ ] Make a fire.
- [ ] Walk down to the river.
- [ ] Look up. The dog is sitting opposite you.
- [ ] Roll in the line.
- [ ] You hear a dog howl.
- [ ] Take your fishing rod.
- [ ] Throw out the line.
- [ ] Throw the dog a piece of fish.
- [ ] Cook the fish.
- [ ] There's a big fish on it.
- [ ] There's a sharp pull.

The birthday party

Do and Understand – © This edition Addison Wesley Longman Limited 1996

The birthday party

Tick the correct sentences.

☐ dancing.
☐ singing.
☐ making a cake.
Start

☐ The girl falls.
☐ You and the girl fall.
☐ You fall and hurt your leg.

☐ goes away.
The girl ☐ helps you up.
☐ starts laughing.

☐ Sit down on a sofa.
☐ Sit down on a chair.
☐ Lie down on the floor.

☐ your head.
Hold ☐ the leg of a chair.
☐ your leg.

☐ pats your cheek and you blush.
The girl ☐ gives you chocolates.
☐ goes away.

☐ are on your way to school.
You ☐ go to a birthday party.
☐ are in a garden.

☐ Give your present to your friend.
☐ Buy a present.
☐ Open the present.

☐ an apple.
Have ☐ some chips.
☐ some orange juice.

☐ sandwich.
Have a ☐ piece of cake.
☐ hamburger.

☐ Switch on the radio.
☐ Catch the ball.
☐ Clap your hands to the music.

☐ Ask a girl to dance with you.
☐ Say good-bye to the girl.
☐ Help the girl.

Going for a walk

Do and Understand – © This edition Addison Wesley Longman Limited 1996

Going for a walk

Colour each sentence in a different colour.

THE SUN IS SHINING IT IS A BEAUTIFUL DAY GO FOR A WALK WHAT'S THAT YOU CAN HEAR A ROLL OF THUNDER THERE ARE BIG BIG BLACK CLOUDS IN THE SKY IT STARTS POURING DOWN RUN HOME YOUR HAIR GETS WET YOUR SHOES GET WET YOUR JEANS GET WET YOUR SHIRT GETS WET YOUR NECK GETS WET YOUR FACE GETS WET YUCK

BOW AND ARROW

Do and Understand – © This edition Addison Wesley Longman Limited 1996

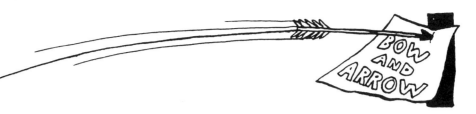

Match the sentence halves.

Say hello	bush in your garden.
They are having	a bow.
Take out your	on the string.
Cut a stick from the	to your neighbours.
Take a piece	your neighbour's chocolate cake.
Make	stick from the bush.
Cut a small	up in the sky.
Make an	tea in their garden.
Put it	comes down.
Shoot it high	of string.
The arrow	arrow.
It lands in	pocket knife.

Swapping

Do and Understand – © This edition Addison Wesley Longman Limited 1996

Swapping

Fill in the missing letters.

You h**e**ar the p__stman.

R__n to the le__ter box.

There is a letter fo__ your m__ther.

T__ke the letter to yo__r mother.

She opens the __nvelope and puts it on the t__ble.

T__ke the __cissors and __ut out the stamps.

Put the stam__s in your scho__lbag.

Leav__ for s__hool.

It's lunch ti__e. Get out your s__ndwich.

Your fr__end has got a big app__e.

S__ap the stamp__ for the apple.

Ea__ the apple.

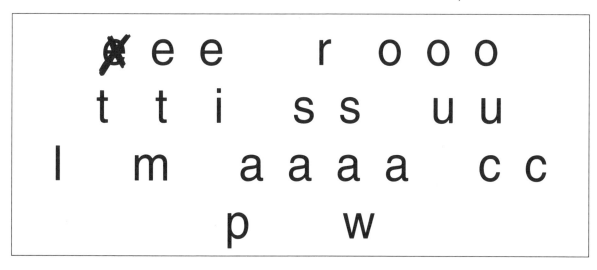

Fill in the words from the box.

Your _____ gives you a shopping list.

_____ a basket.

Get your _____ from the garage.

Jump on _____ .

One pedal _____ off.

Get your _____ bike.

It has got a flat _____ .

Walk to the _____ .

_____ all the things on your list.

Carry them _____ .

You are _____ .

Your mother _____ you a big bowl of ice cream.

　Yummy.

```
          brother's     Take      it      tyre

  bike      mother      hot     comes         home

          shop      Buy      gives
```

The new girl

Do and Understand – © This edition Addison Wesley Longman Limited 1996

Write the correct numbers in the pictures.

1   There is a new girl with her dog in the park.
2   She has got brown eyes and a pony tail.
3   You walk on your hands.
4   The girl looks at you, but she doesn't smile.
5   Run over to the sweet shop.
6   Buy a lolly.
7   Walk over to the girl.
8   There is another boy next to her.
9   He is giving her an ice cream.
10   She takes the ice cream and begins to eat it.
11   She smiles at the other boy.
12   Give the lolly to the girl's dog.

ONLY THREE HOURS ..

Do and Understand – © This edition Addison Wesley Longman Limited 1996

Going by plane

Colour each sentence in a different colour.

SAY GOODBYE TO YOUR FRIENDS PUT YOUR BAG IN THE X RAY MACHINE

PUT THE SEAT BELT ON LEAN BACK SMILE IN THREE HOURS TIME YOU'LL BE HOME

AND PUT YOUR BAG IN THE OVERHEAD LOCKER SIT DOWN

GET ON THE PLANE PUT YOUR BAG

PICK UP YOUR BAG

SHOW YOUR BOARDING PASS

YOUR SISTER

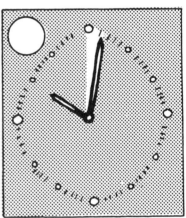

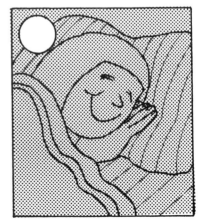

YOUR SISTER

Number the pictures in the box below.

You are going to bed (1).
Your sister (2) is in the bathroom (3).
Go into the kitchen (4).
Open (5) the fridge (6).
Take out some ice (7).
Take the ice to your sister's room.
Put the ice under the cover (8).
Go into your room and listen (9) at the door (10).
A minute (11) passes.
You can hear your sister scream (12).
Jump (13) into bed (14).
Switch off the light (15) and close your eyes (16).

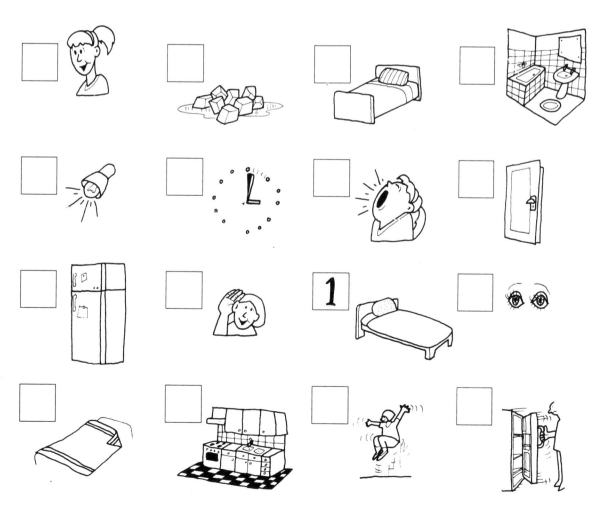

Mineral water

Do and Understand – © This edition Addison Wesley Longman Limited 1996

Mineral water

Put the sentences in the correct order.
Write the numbers in the boxes.

☐ Put the bottle on the table.

☐ Whoosh.

☐ You are thirsty.

☐ Fill all the glasses.

☐ Take a bottle from the fridge.

☐ Your family are having dinner.

☐ Stand up.

☐ Unscrew it.

☐ Wipe your face.

☐ The bottle of mineral water is empty.

☐ Go into the kitchen.

☐ Rock the bottle like a baby.

STORY 31 The mask

Do and Understand – © This edition Addison Wesley Longman Limited 1996

STORY 31 The mask

Tick the correct picture and read the story.

Cut out the ☐ ☐ ☐ .

Hold it ☐ ☐ ☐ your face.

☐ ☐ ☐ into your mum and dad's bedroom.

☐ ☐ ☐ "Argh . . . "

Your mum and dad look very white.

Get your mum and dad a ☐ ☐ of coffee.

Get a piece of ☐ ☐ ☐

Get some colour ☐ ☐ ☐

Draw a ☐ ☐ ☐

Draw a big ☐ ☐ ☐ with warts.

Draw an ugly mouth with big ☐ ☐ ☐

Make two holes for the ☐ ☐ ☐

STORY 32 Going t👦 a fancy dress party

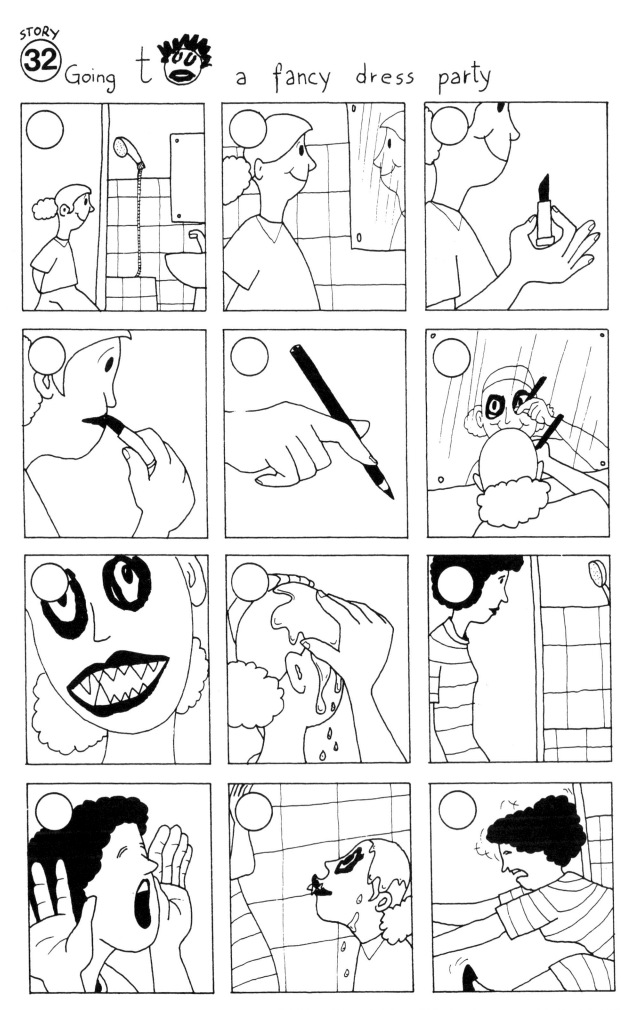

Do and Understand – © This edition Addison Wesley Longman Limited 1996

32 Going t a fancy dress party

Write the correct numbers in the pictures.

1   Go into the bathroom.
2   Stand in front of the mirror.
3   Take some lipstick.
4   Put it on.
5   Take a black pencil.
6   Draw black circles round your eyes.
7   Put your Dracula teeth in your mouth.
8   Put green colour on your hair.
9   Your mother comes into the bathroom.
10 She screams.
11 You want to kiss her.
12 She runs out of the bathroom.

Do and Understand – © This edition Addison Wesley Longman Limited 1996

The bird

Tick the correct words.

You feel
- [ ] scared
- [ ] happy and sad.
- [ ] angry

You start
- [ ] writing
- [ ] reading your story.
- [ ] singing

It's about a
- [ ] cat.
- [ ] flower.
- [ ] man.

He aims his
- [ ] gun
- [ ] knife at a bird.
- [ ] plate

A big
- [ ] tree
- [ ] ant sees this and bites the man's
- [ ] cuts

- [ ] apple.
- [ ] cheese
- [ ] leg.

The man says, "Ouch!" and the bird
- [ ] swims
- [ ] flies away.
- [ ] looks

Your teacher tells you to
- [ ] read a story.
- [ ] sing a song.
- [ ] write a story.

You look out of the
- [ ] door.
- [ ] car.
- [ ] window.

You can see a bird on a
- [ ] tree.
- [ ] table.
- [ ] chair.

Suddenly you
- [ ] eat
- [ ] hear the bang of a gun.
- [ ] chair

The bird
- [ ] falls
- [ ] picks down on the ground.
- [ ] cuts

A man with a
- [ ] pencil
- [ ] gun picks up the bird.
- [ ] book

STORY 34 GRANDPA

Do and Understand – © This edition Addison Wesley Longman Limited 1996

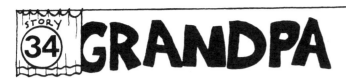

34 GRANDPA

Put the story together again. Match the boxes.

You knock at	on the table.
You listen.	strange noise.
You open the door.	into the kitchen.
Grandpa's glasses are	There is grandpa.
The newspaper	Nothing.
You look	kidnapped your grandpa.
You hear a	grandpa's door.
Monsters! Monsters have	noise again from behind the curtains.
You run	is on the chair.
Father comes	No grandpa there.
You can hear the strange	back with you.
You open the curtains.	around.

In a hurry

Do and Understand – © This edition Addison Wesley Longman Limited 1996

In a hurry

Fill in the missing letters.

Look at your w_a_tch.

You are in a h__rry.

R__n to the b__s stop.

You see s__me stickers in a s__op wind__w.

G__ into the shop and pic__ up the stickers.

You see a m__n ta__king to the shop assistant.

St__re at the m__n's neck.

The man put__ his hands on his neck and stop__

    t__lking.

Pa__ for the stickers.

Star__ at the man's n__ck again and __in__ twi__e.

The m__n look__ conf__sed.

Sm__le at h__m and s__y good-bye.

u u u u   h   o o o

i i   a̶ a a a a a a a

k k   l   w   s s s

c   y   e e

THE MAN IN THE MOON

Do and Understand – © This edition Addison Wesley Longman Limited 1996

THE MAN IN THE MOON

Fill in the words from the box.

You are _____ in your bed.

The _____ is shining through your window.

Suddenly the Man in the Moon is in your _____.

He _____ your hand.

You _____ on your jeans and T-shirt.

You _____ into a spaceship.

He _____ you to the moon.

There are lots of _____.

They are _____ rock 'n' roll.

You dance _____ them.

Suddenly you hear a _____.

You _____.

It's the _____ clock.

You get out of _____.

You are _____ your jeans and T-shirt.

listen	noise	alarm	with	room
get	asleep	takes	dancing	moon
bed	takes	put	people	wearing

AT THE SEASIDE

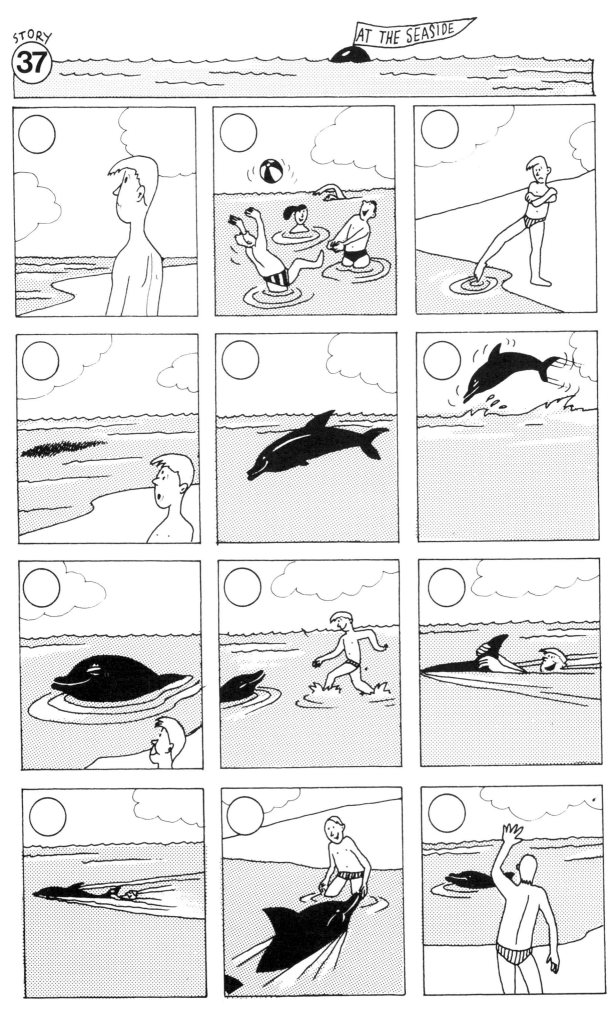

Do and Understand – © This edition Addison Wesley Longman Limited 1996

AT THE SEASIDE

Tick the correct sentences.

☐ It smiles at the boy.
☐ It eats the boy's sandwich.
☐ It swims away.

☐ The boy runs away.
☐ The boy gets on his bike.
☐ The boy runs into the water.

☐ He puts his hand in the dolphin's mouth.
☐ He holds on to the dolphin's fin.
☐ He looks at the dolphin.

☐ He glides through the water with the dolphin.
☐ He swims behind the dolphin.
☐ He runs into the water.

Then the dolphin
☐ eats the boy.
☐ swims away.
☐ brings him back to the beach.

The boy
☐ holds on to the dolphin's fin.
☐ is looking at his friends.
☐ waves good-bye.

☐ A boy is looking at his dog.
☐ A boy is looking at the sea.
☐ A girl is looking at the sea.

His friends are
☐ swimming and playing with a ball.
☐ playing football.
☐ playing with a dolphin.

He is
☐ happy.
☐ angry.
☐ scared of the sea.

Suddenly
☐ the boy can hear a bird.
☐ the boy can see a snake.
☐ he can see a dark shadow.

It's
☐ a dolphin.
☐ a bird.
☐ a boat.

☐ It creeps into the water.
☐ It jumps out of the water.
☐ It waves good-bye.

Chasing wasps

Do and Understand – © This edition Addison Wesley Longman Limited 1996

Chasing Wasps

Fill in the missing words.

Get a _____ of orange juice.

Sit down at the _____ in the _____.

Drink the _____ _____.

A _____ flies into the _____.

Pick up a _____.

_____ _____ and chase the _____ away.

Two _____ circle your _____.

Chase them _____.

_____ wasps _____ you.

Put the glass _____ the table.

_____, "Aaah!"

_____ away.

Stand up	newspaper	glass	garden
attack	glass	away	table	on
orange juice	Ten	wasp	Shout
head	wasps	wasp	Run

Do and Understand – © This edition Addison Wesley Longman Limited 1996

The treasure

Fill in the missing letters.

One night you dream o__ __reasure.

The __ext __ay you __et into your __oat.

Yo__ row t__ a__ island.

You ta__e your spade and wal__ to a __ree.

You __egi__ t__ di__.

A__ter t__ree hours you fee__ very tired.

You lie down a__d go to __leep.

You ha__e another d__eam.

The treasure __ __ in your mother's ove__.

You run to your boa__ and row ho__e.

At home you l__ __k into the oven.

There is your trea__ure: Roas__ chicken. Yumm__.

t	o	o	d	g	o	f
s	k	f	n	l	t	o	g
n	b	n	n	t	s	n
u	r	b	t	v	y	m
	k	h	s	i		

The Pic nic

Do and Understand – © This edition Addison Wesley Longman Limited 1996

The Picnic

Number the words in the box below.

Take a 1 .

Put in a 2 .

Put in some 3 , some 4 , some 5 , some

6 and a 7 .

Take your 8 and go to the countryside.

Stop.

Take out the blanket and sit down.

Eat and 9 . Yummy ! It's wonderful.

You are 10 .

You fall asleep.

You 11 of a beautiful 12 .

There's a big 13 in the lake.

It splashes 14 at you.

Your 15 gets wet.

You open your 16 .

It's raining.

1 basket	dream	bread	face
knife	eyes	butter	bike	cheese
water	blanket	fish	tired	drink
	lake	orange juice		

Write the story.

home.   You   alone   at   are

are   hungry.   very   You

take   fridge.   some   You   the   from   milk

Mmh.   Drink.

cornflakes.   some   You   find

Yummy.   cornflakes.   Eat   some

big   a   bowl.   Take

milk   Pour   cornflakes   the   bowl.   into   and

an apple,   a banana,   a pear and   a peach.   Get

fruit   Cut   the   up.

Taste   everything.   a   of   bit

fruit   into   bowl.   Put   the   the

spoon.   a   Get

to   Sit   eat.   down.

You   feel   don't   now.   hungry

Pick   up   bowl   the   put   and   fridge.   the   in   it

DOWN THE RIVER

Do and Understand – © This edition Addison Wesley Longman Limited 1996

Write the story.

The young magician

Do and Understand – © This edition Addison Wesley Longman Limited 1996

The young magician

Cross out the words that do not belong to the story.
Write the story using the words from the box.

The old policeman leaves the house.

The hungry girl opens the door.

She takes out a little book.

She opens the book and begins to sing.

Then she gets a glass.

She reads aloud from the book.

Suddenly there is a little pink cake in the glass.

When she eats it, the cake gets bigger and bigger.

The hungry girl shouts, "Hurray".

But the cake is very big now.

Then the old policeman comes home.

He starts dancing.

Then he sings some magic songs.

The cake gets smaller again.

The girl and the old policeman sit down and eat it.

words	bigger	magician	touches
magician	he	magician	He
wonderful	plate	cupboard	young
He	young	smaller	He
magician	read	laughing	small
man	castle	boy	big	plate
smaller	Stop	on	says	he

Eating spaghetti

Cross out the words that do not belong to the story.
Write the story using the words from the box.

Go to a park.
Sit down at a swimming pool.
Call the teacher and order spaghetti.
The teacher brings the pizza.
He laughs and drops the spaghetti.
Wipe the spaghetti off your face.
The waiter brings you another plate of mushrooms.
Start singing.
There's spaghetti on the wall.
There's spaghetti on the chair.
But there's no spaghetti in your ears.
Call the waiter and ask for a watch.
The waiter brings you a banana.
Cut the spaghetti.
Eat it with your fingers.
Wonderful spaghetti.

table	eating	falls	restaurant
table	floor	spaghetti	waiter
trousers	mouth	spaghetti	waiter
knife	knife	spoon	

Fill in the words from the box.

Open your maths _____.

Try to _____.

Get a _____.

Sharpen a _____.

You _____ hungry.

Get a sandwich from the _____.

Look again at your maths _____.

Put a _____ into your cassette recorder.

Listen to the cassette.

You feel _____.

Get a glass of _____ from the kitchen.

Switch on the _____.

Watch _____.

Listen. You can _____ your dad.

Switch _____ the TV.

Say, "Dad, _____ me with my maths homework please."

book	feel	TV	concentrate
sharpener	milk	pencil	hear
kitchen	homework		thirsty
cassette	off	help	TV

Little green men

Write the story.

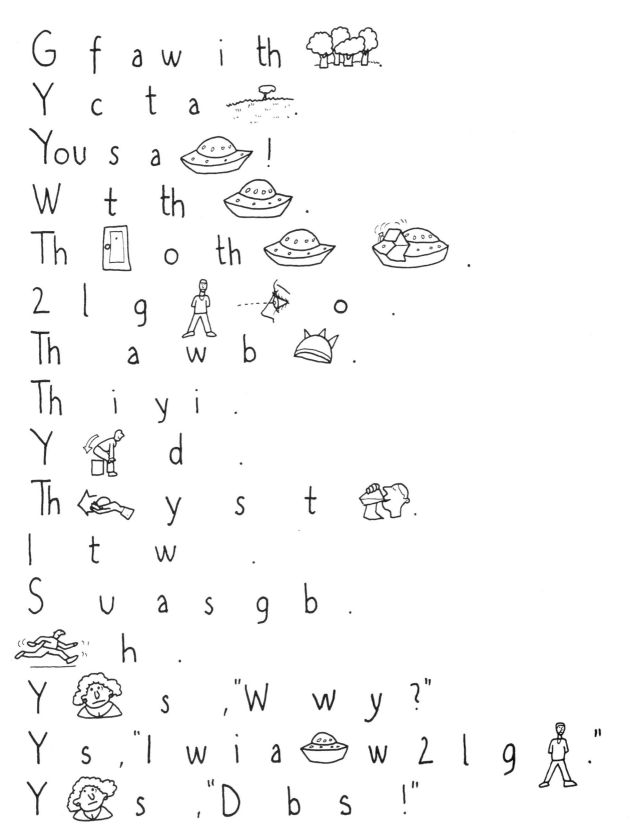

The balloon

Do and Understand – © This edition Addison Wesley Longman Limited 1996

The balloon

Colour the balloons that go together in the same colour.
Then write the story.

Do and Understand – © This edition Addison Wesley Longman Limited 1996

Chasing a monster

Write the story.

It's a | Sunday | night. | Monday | evening. | Tuesday | morning.

Shout, | "Come in." | "Hello." | "Get out."

Shout, "Stop! You can have some | comics." | cornflakes." | paper."

The monster is | brown. | green. | black | It has | silver | golden | fingernails | grey | eyes, | pink | blue | eyes | and | green | teeth. | yellow | white | ears | orange

The | cupboard | open. | door | is | broken | window | brown.

Take the | spaghetti | soup | away. | cornflakes

Your | cats | asleep. | dogs | are | hungrey. | parents | tired.

You can hear your | cats | scream. | dogs | sing. | parents | laugh.

The | monster | jumps up and runs upstairs. | dog | cat

You | look | after | shout | at | the monster. | run | into

Jump | look | kitchen. | Go | into the | bedroom. | Get | bathroom.

Jump | car. | Look | out of the | door. | Climb | window.

You | look | run | into their bedroom. | go

You can | feel | dog | climb | nose. | hear | the | mouse | run | your dad's | garden. | see | monster | eat | car.

There is a | hamster | sitting | in | table | fly | dancing | at | the | bed | eating | soup. | monster | sleeping | under | cupboard | spaghetti. | cornflakes.

They | angry. | You | feel | hungry. | I | tried.

Superboy

Do and Understand – © This edition Addison Wesley Longman Limited 1996

wood. in Superboy a is walking

walks a He pool. to

girl. He is crying. She a sees

is into water. She looking the

water. the Superboy into looks

He see golden crown. can a

into water. the Superboy dives

picks He the up crown.

swims Then girl. he the to

her crown. the gives He

girl kisses Superboy. The

noise. loud is a There Boom.

changes Superboy a horse. into

horse gets girl The away. and rides the on

TREASURE HUNT

Do and Understand – © This edition Addison Wesley Longman Limited 1996

TREASURE HUNT

Find the sentences and write the story.

		Get out of		
the boat		You find a		
You are	is on top of	The castle		
	a castle on a small		Open the	
Row to		reading in a		
Take your		very old piece of		
	a boat.		your book.	
paper with a drawing in	The treasure is in		There is	
	castle's big	of paper in		
it.	bike and ride to		cellar.	
	very old book.		"Well done."	
the island.	a box.	look for the		
			the sea.	Get into
	a treasure map.		gate.	
	a big hill.			
small island.		There's a piece		
		Take an atlas and		
Go down		It's		
		Open		
island in the sea.		it.	into the	
	It says,